All These Little Stars

by
Nicole Zamlout

Published by

Copyright 2021 Nicole Zamlout.

All rights reserved.

Published by Read Furiously. First Edition.

ISBN – 978-1-7337360-9-1

Poetry
Young Adult Poetry
Constelation Poetry
Poetry Collection – Single Author
Women Writers

In accordance with the U.S. Copyright Act of 1979, the scanning, uploading, and electronic sharing of any part of this book without the permission of the publisher or creator is forbidden.

For more information on *All These Little Stars* or Read Furiously, please visit readfuriously.com. For inquiries, please contact samantha@readfuriously.com.

Edited by Samantha Atzeni

Read (v): The act of interpreting and understanding the written word.

Furiously (adv): To engage in an activity with passion and excitement.

Read Often. Read Well.
Read Furiously

For my family, my friends, and the stars
that kept me going

Table of Contents

Debut
1

Of Concrete Deserts and Young Love
4

Color Me in Love
6

Snapshots
38

9,100km
40

Too Many Murders (of Crows)
52

Skeletal Storyteller
48

H.D.D.
62

Swallow
72

Dancing with Devils and Other Such Nonsense
76

Shower Thoughts
80

Pocket-Sized Gods
82

All These Little Stars
88

Fin
91

Debut

I suppose I should start with some kind of witty remark, or go on about my inspiration for this book, begin where beginnings lie.

I was never much for standards though.

The fact is that this book you hold now is here because I've had the writing bug crawling under my skin since I was small.

That's all you're getting for now. I've always been a believer in leaving others to want more, leaving breadcrumbs behind for others to follow.

So, allow me to drop the crumbs, and allow yourself to roll up your sleeves and follow.

I promise to make it worth your while.

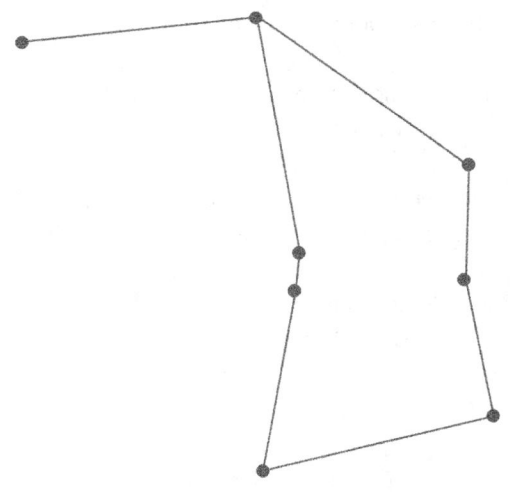

This first one is a bit short but is a personal favorite.

This one was from my mind wondering about love, specifically first meetings.

Why do we stick to only certain scenarios?

Like a school hallway or a concert or some other big event where the world is already a whirlwind?

Love is one on its own, isn't it? It sets the heart into a triple motion rollercoaster-esque sweep that it remains in for as long or as short it lasts.

It's momentous enough without the pomp and circumstance of the world outside its cage of bone.

So why can't it begin anywhere, even a parking lot on a hot day?

For these two, it did.

(And maybe I was just writing a letter to the universe to set my heart on this course because I was tired of waiting in concrete deserts for the sweep to come.)

Of Concrete Deserts and Young Love

I saw you in a parking lot.

You were leaning against the wall of the CVS, just staring at the clouds, watching the world go by. The asphalt was scorching under my feet as I came over to you. Your smile was fuller than that noonday sun, and I understood why you hid. So she wouldn't be jealous.

You were always considerate like that.

I remember all the stupid things we'd say to each other. Like how we would fight off a thousand snails to get each other back. Or how we would endure the worst bad breath in order to see the other smile. We were a couple of weirdos, but when we made love it was everything any author could hope for. It was ink stained fingers, tracing the blurry outlines of each other until they became clear again. It was holding each other until the Sun melted us because she never forgot her jealousy. It was smiling so wide that our lips cried in protest at the abuse, only for them to fall on ears too full of each other's heartbeats to care or listen.

It was the kind of young love that is never supposed to last. And it didn't. It ended in a blaze of glory, your hand leaving mine as your family drove away. You cried out as your car turned the curb how we would find each other again, across fields of garbage and landmines. How we would fight the smell and fear for another kiss. I think you said that because you knew this would be your last sight of me, and you wanted me to be smiling. So then when you thought of me, you could convince yourself that I'm better off without you.

I'm not, if you're wondering. Because you took my heart with you when you left.

And I would cross every concrete desert, just to tell you that you can keep it.

On that note, we see a lot of love stories that adhere to cliché nowadays, don't we?

Person A meets Person B, they fall in love, go through drama, etc. ad nauseam.

I always hated that formula.

Don't get me wrong, some great stories have come from it and I am very guilty of adhering to it with some of my earlier stories.

But then I met a fantastic girl in my choir class who made me ask an important question: why can't love stories be about more than just the couple themselves?

Why can't they, together, learn and grow from each other outside of cute compliments and tense moments?

Why can't one of them simply try to paint with new colors in the other's world, with love being a byproduct rather than the main goal?

With those musings (and a lot of research) this story was born.

I hope it helps break the black-and-white mold love stories have been stuck in.

Color Me In Love

1

For most of my life, color has been in abundance.

It shifted and exploded across my vision, dancing before me in all its wonder. The littlest things create the most spectacular rainbow.

But it wasn't until I met Connor that I truly realized how lovely a colorful world could be.

Because some things in life are only truly wonderful when they are shared.

2

It started last summer.

My little sister Mia came running into my room while I was lying on my bed, reading my favorite book for the fifteenth time: *The Giver* by Lois Lowry.

She ran to me, a burst of bright yellow dancing with her bright smile.

"Iris, Iris! The movers are here!"

I laughed and followed her outside as she bounced out of the room, quick as lightning, the yellow trailing behind her. Mia has been obsessed with the house next door ever since she saw the "For–Sale" sign in June. It was now mid–July, and the sun bounced off the silver roof of the van. Men in grey shirts, already soaked in sweat, were carrying in furniture and boxes inside the house, their authoritative voices showering the afternoon in dark green that burst and move with their hefting arms.

A woman stood outside, occasionally answering questions, allowing dots of bright orange to mix with the green in sharp flashes.

A man, I assumed her husband, walked over to her and kissed her cheek, a warm mahogany color radiating off of him like sunbeams as he spoke softly to her, the colors mixing sweetly like a sunset.

Mia was bouncing with joy as she watched the movers, yellow bouncing with her. My eyes, however, trailed away. Up the house, toward a nearby window.

Where a set of clear blue eyes stared into mine, a dark blue flashing by like a bird.

It was only for a moment, then they were gone.

Synesthesia

A neurological phenomenon in which stimulation of one sensory or cognitive pathway leads to automatic, involuntary experience in a second sensory or cognitive pathway. I.e. colors appear in tandem with words or numbers, numbers elicited locations in space, or numbers appear in a three dimensional map.[1]

Most common form: colors appear in tandem upon hearing words or numbers. Also occurs upon seeing a particular person or saying that person's name.

---

[1] *A quote from the Wikipedia entry on Synesthesia. Cytowic, Richard E. (2002). Synesthesia: A Union of the Senses (2nd ed.). Cambridge, Massachusetts: MIT Press.*

Color Blindness

A decreased ability to see color or differences in color. People with complete color blindness may have decreased visual acuity. I.e. uncomfortable in brightly-lit environments.

(Keep these in mind.)

4

Walking has always been a nice experience for me.

I don't just see the trees, the birds, the people.

I see the shades of each birdsong, from wild yellow to mellow purple, an array of colors mixing like a living rainbow that danced and swung from each corner of the park.

I see the sweet sound of lovers whispering to each other, shades of pink and red dancing in the air in joy and soft languor, pirouetting through the trees like gentle ballerinas.

I see the rustle of the trees, the light and dark green creating the loveliest contrast as they sway along to the silent beat of nature whose colors always never stay the same.

I could stare for hours.

"Penny for your thoughts?"

I jump, turn, and am greeted by those clear blue eyes again. The voice is the nicest shade of royal blue I've ever seen. I blink my iridescent eyes (the ones that gave me my name) at him, processing the question as I take him in.

His hair is a nice mossy brown, long enough to reach the nap of his neck. His face has a slight tan to it, with a roman nose and a wide smile. He's tall, lanky, but seems fit. Despite the weather, he's wearing a black T-shirt, a black hoodie, black jeans, and black sneakers. All the dark colors cannot erase the bright blue of him, dancing and joining the chorus of color the park has each day.

He smiles shyly at me, waving a hand, the blue doing a somersault. "Hello?"

I smile at him. "Just looking at the colors."

He raises an eyebrow. Laughing, I stick out my hand.

"Hi, I'm Iris. Yes, after the rainbow goddess from Greek myth. I have synesthesia, so I see colors in pretty much everything."

He takes my hand with a smirk.

"It's nice to meet you, Iris. I'm Connor. Yes, I am aware that I'm in all black in the middle of July and I don't care. Yes, I know I'll bake to death and I am perfectly fine with that."

I quirk a brow. "Are you looking to be golden brown or over easy?" He shrugs, the blue twirling off his shoulders like steam. "Haven't decided yet."

"Seeing how the day goes?"

"Yup, never know if it ends up being a burnt day."

We end up laughing pretty loudly at each other's introductions and our silly repertoire. The royal blue of his voice wiggled as he laughs, making me smile. My stomach does little flip flops at seeing him so unabashed.

"So, this is what people do for fun around here? Walk and look at trees?"

I shrug, my hot pink bouncing like an excited puppy. "It's what I do. I also draw."

He smiles again. "Me too. Charcoal mostly."

"Oil and paints," I reply. He nods approvingly.

"CONNOR!"

From across the street, the woman I saw yesterday shouts to us, her orange overpowering the colors of the park for a moment, proud and unashamed. Connor turns and smiles.

"Be there in a second, Mom!" he calls back, the blue slipping back toward her.

She smiles at him. He gets his smile from her. "Don't think just because you've made a new friend you can get out of helping us unpack!"

With that, she walks back into the house, trailing bright orange behind her as it fades, the colors of the park resuming their concert.

He turns to me, slightly sheepish. "I got to go. It was nice meeting you."

"Wait!" I call after a second, my pink radiating off of me in my determination. He turns back, a question on his face, blue curling around his hair.

I take out my phone and open the Contact app. I hold it out to him in silent invitation.

He smiles, takes it, and punches in his number. I text him a rainbow emoji so he has mine. He chuckles, raising an eyebrow in a "really?" pose before he walks off, leaving that lovely royal blue and my racing heart behind.

5

To Connor
From Iris
   Hey! How r u?

To Iris
From Connor
   Exhausted from moving boxes. SOS! Need rescuing before tomorrow! That's when the patio furniture gets here!

I couldn't help the giggle that bubbled out of me, a little puff of hot pink.

To Connor
From Iris
   Don't worry. I'll spring you ;)

To Iris
From Connor
   U r a life saver.

To Connor
From Iris
   I try ;)

To Iris
From Connor
   LOL. U know, idk anything about you. Except you like walking and painting.

To Connor
From Iris
The same case could be said for you, mister. ;)

BTW I use a lot of winkie faces.

To Iris
From Connor
> That was very evident. But anyway, I want to get to know you little better.

I bit my lip, nervous and excited, pink puffing up like a scared chick.

To Connor
From Iris
> 20 ?s anyone?

To Iris
From Connor
> Sure. Ladies first ;)

To Connor
From Iris
> Favorite food?

To Iris
From Connor
> Pizza. U?

To Connor
From Iris
> Sushi.

To Iris
From Connor
> Future dreams?

To Connor
From Iris
> Become a painter. Travel the world. U?

To Iris
From Connor
> Same here. It's the dream!

To Connor
From Iris
> LOL IKR. Ok, dogs or cats?

To Iris
From Connor
> Cats. U?

To Connor
From Iris
> Same. Dogs are nice, just little too nice.

To Iris
From Connor
> I get that. Ummm favorite book?

To Connor
From Iris
> *The Giver* by Lois Lowry

To Iris
From Connor
> I've been meaning to read that. Mine's *Harry Potter and the Half Blood Prince*. The intrigue of that one always gets me excited.

To Connor
From Iris
> Me 2! It's so good.
>
> Ummmmm favorite color?

He didn't answer for a minute. I don't know why, but I felt like I had said something wrong.

To Iris
From Connor
    I gtg. Goodnight.

Now I know something is wrong, my pink now curling like sour milk. But what did I say?

6

That was the question that buzzed in my mind as I stood at the door of Connor's house. The bell, a pleasant chime, bouncing off the walls, a faint red ball bouncing through the house like a loyal dog. Connor's mother answered the door, smiling widely at my sheepish expression.

"Hello. I'm Iris. I'm here to see Connor."

"I figured. I saw the two of you talking yesterday. Come in, come in."

She waved me inside the sitting room, a cross between elegant and messy with nice furniture surrounded by cardboard boxes. She called up the stairs, a burst of orange slipping over the scenery like a mist. "Connor! Your friend is here!" He walked down the stairs, his footsteps light despite his heavy shoes. Once again, he was in all black, the blue hanging like a funeral shroud.

I shuffled my feet. His mom vanished into the kitchen. Connor looked at me with a mix of apprehension and something that looked like hope, the blue bouncing nervously.

"Wanna take a walk?" I asked him nervously. He smiled, a little twitch of his lips as he nodded, the blue uncoiling from his shoulders. We went out the front door, into the day full of revelations.

7
■ ■ ■ ■ ■

The sun slipped down on the sidewalk in soft, multicolored waves as we walked, the colors of the mid-day sun mixing with the softly bobbing colors of the park and those returning from their daily adventures.

The sidewalk turned to grass, the colors shifting subtly over our heads and under our feet as we neared some of the trees.

I took a deep breath. "So......"

He coughed, awkwardly, his blue curling back toward him, spruce to mirror his, why was he afraid? "So."

I finally relented. "If I said something to offend you, I'm sorry."

He.... laughed.

It was a short, bitter thing, a dark slate that assaulted the spruce, making me cringe.

"You didn't say anything to offend me. I was just weird yesterday." He squinted a little as we stepped out of the shade and back into the multicolored sunlight, his spruce darkening further, bits of indigo peeking through.

I raised an eyebrow. Something was amiss.

Suddenly, everything came together. The dark clothes, the charcoals, the squinting.

"Oh."

He must have seen the realization on my face, because he nodded, the blue almost faded now into a stone shade.

"I'm completely colorblind."

Hearing it out loud made my gut twist. "I..."

He raised his hand, the indigo curling and sharpening, ready for a fight. "Please don't apologize. I don't want sympathy and you didn't know. It's fine."

I wanted to argue, to close the riff that seemed to have opened between us. But I knew talking would just make it worse. So, I nodded.

Friends always were a bit tricky for me. They aren't colors with neat meanings and names. So, like always, I misinterpreted the meaning and filled in the wrong shade, leaving me with unhappy hues and missed rainbows.

We walked in silence for another minute or two, the indigo still sharper than any blade. Then, he whispered "The light is starting to hurt my eyes. I'll see you later."

He crossed back to his house, leaving a trail of dark grey that settled into the blue like a parasite. One of the few colors he could see.

8

That night, my mind was wracked with guilt and contemplation, the pink now a crepe shade wrapped in stressed packages around me.

How was I going to fix this? Was there even anything I could do, any colors I can use to counteract the mistaken choice of shade? I didn't know. Like always, I had mistaken one color for another, so wrapped up in the little world of hues that made up my life. I just hope the right one will pop up, leading me to a new rainbow that will fix this.

My phone pinged, the crepe spiking back to life into strawberry.

To Iris
From Connor
>Hey, you there?

I was shocked. I stared at my phone, frozen, the strawberry swirling until another ping startled me, sending it flying around me.

To Iris
From Connor
>Hellllllloooooooooo! Is anybody out theeeeeerrrrrreeeee?

I giggled, the strawberry calming to my usual hot pink, puffs now floating aimlessly.

To Connor
From Iris
>LOL. Hi.

To Iris
From Connor
>I'm sorry about today. It's just......you're the first person I've told besides my parents. It's a touchy subject.

To Connor
From Iris
>I get it. It's ok. We don't have to talk about it.

To Iris
From Connor
>Is it weird that I want to? I know you have synesthesia, so it's different for you too.
>
>Seeing colors everywhere must be nice.

My heart clenched at that last sentence, the pink sinking. Then, inspiration struck.

To Connor
From Iris
> I could teach you.

To Iris
From Connor
> Come again?????

To Connor
From Iris
> I could tell you what colors look like based on what I see and know.
>
> Unless you don't want to.
>
> I don't want to make you sad.

To Iris
From Connor
> That......would actually be nice.
>
> I'm in.

I am not ashamed to say that I squealed, the pink flashing in joy.

To Connor
From Iris
> Great! Rest up. Tomorrow is your color education!

To Iris
From Connor
> Can't wait! :)

9

I waited patiently under the tree nearby his house the next day. He walked out with a certain spring in his step, his royal blue shifting to a lighter shade, bouncing happily in time with him.

"Ok. Where are we going?" he said in a cheery tone, the baby blue bobbing happily.

I just gestured for him to follow me. We walked alongside each other, just taking in the view of the park, the colors melting and swirling in their usual concert.

"Alrighty. So, I'm just going to go in order. First the primary colors. Then secondary. We will start with red."

We stopped at a bench and sat down. I was silent for a minute and wracked my brain for a good example, my pink dancing in thought around me. Finally, one surfaced.

"You know how, you get angry at someone? Like super angry? Steam feels like it will pour out of your ears, your face scrunches up, your fists are balled? That's one type of red. It's dark, mean."

The wine color surfaces for a moment by my hand, the hypothetical emotion creating the sticky shade.

Connor nods, gesturing for me to continue, the blue prancing with his movements.

"Have you ever felt so happy that you want to scream wildly, for no reason? That's another kind of red. It's lighter, brighter."

The raspberry hue pops up by my mouth, brighter than a sunrise and happy as can be.

Connor moved closer to me, out of the glare of the sun, closer to me in the shade of the tree next to the bench.

My stomach flipped. The royal blue of him was warm, soft, curling like a lazy cat around his shoulders.

"Have you ever been so embarrassed about something? You feel all uncomfortable and itchy, like bugs are crawling on you? That's another red. It's bright, but not as nice to look at." The blush color dusts just over my cheeks, a faded photo of the bright red by my mouth a moment ago.

Connor nodded again, eyes closed, picturing it.

My face felt hot. My skin felt itchy, but pleasantly so. The blush fades only lightly, forming into my pink, pale in shyness. I fidgeted a bit.

Connor smiled. "I can see it. At least, I can imagine it." He opened his eyes, the smile still in place, making the royal blue even brighter.

Making that strange feeling even stronger.

It didn't really have a color, because all I saw was his blue, bouncing in joy over the gift I gave him.

10

That night, the thought of his smile kept me awake.

It also let a smile of my own grow as it danced behind my lids, my pink dancing in time with it.

11

He joins me on my stoop the next day, eating ice cream from the local truck making his rounds.

"So, orange today," I say, finishing off my vanilla soft serve with rainbow sprinkles, my pink wiggling happily at the treat.

Connor nods, polishing off his chocolate soft serve and wiped his hands with the napkin, his blue jerking with the movement. He closes his eyes.

"I'm ready."

I grin evilly, my pink going rouge, swirling in excitement. My hand shoots out and starts tickling his sides, the rouge turning to punch, spiking with my enthusiasm. He squirms and begins to giggle, the blue bouncing faster as it goes on.

"IRIS! IRIS! STOP! AHAHAHAHAH!"

His laughter draws out my own, his royal blue turning cobalt, meeting my punch pink as they both bounce together in joy overhead.

Finally, I stop. He's gasping for air.

"What the heck?!", he asks, breathless, the cobalt shifting back to royal blue, settling by his shoulders again.

I grin. "That's orange. That overly bouncing, giggly feeling you get when tickled."

The apricot shade pops by my stomach, wiggling happily almost like my fingers were a second ago.

He grins, then fidgets a bit, the blue fading a bit in his shyness. Finally, he speaks, not looking at me, blue by his hair.

"Can you tickle me again?"

The way he asks is absolutely adorable, with a sheepish smile and soft tone, the royal blue shifting to cerulean, hiding like a shy puppy.

I do, and his smile wasn't just from the tickling.

"I see it, I see it.", he says in between giggles, cerulean shifting to sky blue, bouncing again overhead.

That makes me smile wider than anything else.

12

Connor rang the doorbell, swaying slightly on his feet in nervousness.

He didn't know why he was nervous. It was Iris, his friend. They were just going to hang out, like they normally did.

Why was he so fidgety?

Maybe because seeing her every day made a strange sensation bubble up in his heart. Maybe because every time she taught him about a new color, he felt like he could actually see it. Maybe because she had become color to him, bright and varied.

He shook the thoughts away. Before he could scold himself, the door sprang open.

A little girl, no more than ten, ran right to him and wrapped her little arms around his waist. Her smile was radiant as he stumbled back from the momentum.

"Hello," he said shyly, wondering what was going on but not opposed to getting a hug from the cute child.

"Hi! I'm Mia. What's your name?" she asked, her wide eyes imploring.

"I'm Connor. I'm a friend of your sister. Is she home?" he asked, poking his head in the doorway.

"Ok Mia, off. He needs to breathe." Iris came outside, a soft smile on her face as she got the girl to remove herself from him.

There went his heart again.

"Wanna play with your bubbles outside while we talk?" Iris asked the girl, who nodded vigorously. Iris giggled, kissed the top of her head, and quickly ducked inside. She came back with a small bottle. Mia squealed in delight, grabbing the bottle and running outside.

Connor looked at Iris and lifted a brow. "You had something to do with that."

Iris feigned innocence. "Me? No."

She smiled a moment later.

"Well, maybe. She wanted to meet the person I have been spending so much time with. Also, she's our example for today."

Connor looked slightly confused at her.

"Yellow. She's a bright, lovely yellow."

Connor sat down next to Iris on the steps, watching the child play happily with her bubbles, running after them as they danced in the air.

Connor closed his eyes, the little girl's smile and laugh echoing in his mind. A faint connection clicked in his head. He thought he saw a wisp of the bumblebee tone when he opened his eyes again to his normal, fossil tinted world.

It was gone so quickly; he must have imagined it.

Still, he smiled. It was better than nothing.

"I saw it," he whispered, still amazed that he was being taught the one thing everyone told him was impossible to teach.

Irish beamed, and Connor's heart sped up.

Seeing her smile was worth more than all the color to him.

13

We sat at the same bench we did for red when we did green.

Green was going to be difficult. I had very few examples since it came in so many varied forms.

Finally, an idea struck.

"Give me your hands."

Connor opened his eyes, slightly confused, but did nonetheless.

I squeezed them to comfort him, then began.

"Today is a nice summer day. The sun is beating down gently, allowing the trees to bask in its rays. The breeze is shifting each leaf in a soft dance, quiet and sure. I'm here, with you. The world is at peace."

Connor's eyes had slipped closed again as I spoke. He smiled softly, soothed and serene, the fern hue settling happily by our joined hands.

"I saw it," he whispered to me.

We were so close, inches apart. The peace settled over us, something growing alongside of it, the fern becoming sharper now, a more expectant emerald.

We leaned closer.......

"BARK!"

The bark from a nearby Corgi startled us away from each other. Cheeks burning the blush tone I showed him for embarrassment, we sat a comical distance away from each other for a while. Then, quickly, I said "I better go. I have to watch Mia for my mom today. Talk to you later!"

Connor just replied "Bye," before I was off, heart pounding, my pink still blush, twisting itself into happy knots.

A smile forming on my lips.

14

Oh. My. God.

I almost kissed him!!!!

I couldn't stop pacing my room that night, my mind flashing back to that afternoon, my pink all over the room, dancing in joy and confusion.

What was I thinking?

Well, my brain supplied, you were probably thinking of his cute smile that gives you butterflies. Or maybe it was his really sweet laugh? Or perhaps it was his amazing clear blue eyes that shine when you make a joke.....

"Ugh! Stop it!" I yelled at the stream of thoughts, the pink spiking in my annoyance. I flopped in my bed in defeat, wondering what the heck I was going to do now.

My eyes wandered over to my bedside table, where a picture of my dad and I sat happily. Dad worked for a big international company and wasn't home much. When he was, though, he and I had the best time. The picture was of when we went to a nearby farm to pick blueberries and strawberries last summer. That was when he told me about the importance of the color blue......

DING DING DING!!!!

I leapt from my bed and let out a whoop, my pink joining me in my epiphany. Grabbing the picture, I kissed it and smiled widely.

I knew just what to do now. It would be scary, terrifying even. But I knew it was right.

Plus, I now at least had a plan. I count that as something.

15

I shifted on the bench, waiting in anticipation. The sun shone down encouragingly, lighting the world in an array of rainbow light, the dancing greens, reds and pinks shining brighter than usual. The birds chirped happily, highlighting the perfection of the warm, late July day with their lovely blue noted songs.

Connor walked over, his soft, sweet smile appearing as he saw me, his blue happily curled by his shoulders. My stomach did its now familiar somersaults, my pink swirling to meet him.

"Hey," he greeted shyly, tucking some of his long hair behind his ear, where some of his blue now hid.

"Hey," I replied, equally flustered, the red from embarrassment and my flush sitting on my cheeks.

We sat in silence for a minute. The world seemed to hold its breath, colors pausing their dance.

"So," I said a bit too loudly, as if I could spur the worlds back into

motion, my pink radiating out with my shout. "Blue today."
Connor nodded and eagerly closed his eyes, his blue settling from his hair back to his shoulders. I took a deep breath.

Here we go.

"So, when I was younger, I asked my dad how he knew he loved my mom. He smiled and told me how she was wearing a blue shirt when they met, so he knew that they were meant to be. I was confused, of course, and asked what that had to do with it. He told me that blue is the color of love to him. It's pure, honest, soft, a gentle cornflower shade. It symbolizes healing and peace. It also symbolizes power. Blue reminds him that love can have rocky, dark times, shifting from that cornflower to a rough zaffre. But, those times always clear to lovely, light cornflower shades again if you're willing to live with the darker zaffre shades for a while."

As I spoke, the colors danced before me, the cornflower blue shifting to zaffre and back again, right over my heart.

I scooted closer to him, his eyes still closed, blue still by his shoulders.

"When I met you, I saw the most beautiful shade of royal blue I had ever seen. I know you can't see it, but I can, and now whenever I see you, my stomach ties itself up in knots and I can't really think straight, and I get nervous but the good kind of nervous..."

He laughed a little. I blushed, matching my embarrassed blush pink.

"Right, rambling. Anyway, what I'm trying to say is that I really like you, and I hope I don't make things weird if I do this and you don't feel the same way."

I could tell Connor was about to open his eyes and ask what I meant, his royal blue shifting to navy, rushing to his hair in confusion.

I kissed him before he could.

He froze for a moment, navy confusion blue radiating out in shock in a bright electric shade. Then he returned the kiss, settling into royal by his shoulders again.

It was soft, sweet, with a little rockiness to it.

It was blue.

He pulled away for a second to whisper "I see it," before smiling, his blue and the one by my heart making a perfect painting.

We kissed again. And again. And again.

Little mattered after that.

16

To Connor
From Iris
>Hey you. Come over. I have a surprise!

To Iris
From Connor
>Babe.....it's 3 am.
>
>OMG I just called you babe and didn't ask.
>
>IDK if that's ok with you if I call you that or if that's too weird or...

To Connor
From Iris
>Connor. Relax. It's cute and I love it ;)
>
>Also I NEED to see that in person cause I bet its ADORABLE!!!!

To Iris
From Connor
　blushing

To Connor
From Iris
　LOL. Get over here "babe"

To Iris
From Connor
　On my way.

17

Connor glanced around the small roof of Iris's house. She had texted him that his "surprise" was on the roof with her. He was debating texting her again when a figure jumped behind him.

"AH!" he shouted, turning to see a grinning Iris behind him. She was holding back giggles.

He tried to look upset, but his lips quirked up in a smirk.

"Not cool, dude," he told her, a laugh bleeding into his voice.

Iris quirked a brow. "Don't you mean babe?"

"You're never going to let me live that down, are you?"

"Nope," she said to him, popping the "p".

He grinned mischievously then, grabbing her by the hand and giving her a peck on the lips. She smiled and went in for another kiss, this one longer and slower. Connor shivered a little. He had never kissed anyone before Iris, so the sensation was a little overwhelming. In a

good way though.
They parted, smiling dopily.

"Was that my surprise?" he whispered, even though it was only the night air that could hear them.

Iris shook her head and pointed over her shoulder. There, a small brass telescope sat on a blanket. Next to it, another sheet laid, big enough for two people to sit and take turns looking at the stars.

Connor's smile widened. "How did you know I like astronomy?"

Iris brightened. "I asked your mom. I wanted to plan something nice, so I called the house two days ago, after we....."

The sentence went unfinished. There was no need to finish it.

Iris walked him over to the sheet, where the two sat quietly. They gazed at the few stars they could see through the small telescope and the clouded night sky. Connor talked about a few of them, lighting up every time he could spin another story for her. Iris listened with a soft smile. Her eyes fluttered with each passing minute, until she was asleep on Connor's shoulder. He let her rest for a few moments, admiring her quietly. Her little button nose, the quirk of her lips, her dark, pixie cut hair.

She was perfect to him.

If only he could see her in color.

Connor never really wished for that much anymore. Not until he met her. But he had realized something:

He didn't really need the colors to know that she was beautiful.

He smiled at the thought as she stirred slightly. After a moment of blinking the sleep away, the two said their quiet goodbyes. As Connor slipped back into his room, the monochromatic sunrise at his back, he wondered if this what love felt like.

18

We walked quietly along the familiar park path the next day, another perfect picture of a day surrounding us, the colors bouncing along in their content waves.

Swinging our held hands between us, his royal blue and my hot pink tangling together, I wracked my brain for an example of today's color: purple.

Connor started squinting again, so we sat under the shade of a nearby oak tree, its calming green greeting us. After a moment of silence filled in with multicolored birdsong, it came to me.

"Purple is the feeling you get when you sneak out of the house or pull a prank on someone. That dark, excited feeling that churns in your stomach and makes your pulse jump. The feeling that makes you feel more alive than you've ever felt before."

The magenta hue sprang forward as I spoke, hovering over my nose in an excited jumble.

Connor's eyes closed, picturing the scene. His little smirk curled onto his lips, soft and awestruck, his blue curling around him contently.

"I see it."

My heart hammered at the words, my pink spiking with each beat.

He opened his eyes, turning to me with a curious expression, the blue dancing.

"That seems pretty specific. Is there something you want to tell me?"

I laughed at his fake serious expression, my pink a taffy shade that jumped with my voice. "I'm secretly a delinquent. I sneak out to the park when I can't sleep after closing time to take in the night life. I hope you don't think less of me because of my criminal activities."

Connor laughed, full and bright, the blue turning teal, echoing my pink. "I don't mind. I kinda like this dangerous side of you. It's interesting."

We laughed again. Connor leaned over, kissing me on the cheek.

Then the forehead.

Then the tip of my nose.

Each kiss brings the blue with it, an extra kiss.

I giggled and pretended to bat him away and look at the mostly empty park, my pink giving away my rose-tinted happiness with its swirling. "You wild man!"

He laughed, his smile outshining every sun that existed, his blue as vibrant as any sky.

"Only with you."

19

The days wore on like this.

Talking about every color until he could see each one. Or at least imagine what each one looked like.

To him it didn't matter.

We got closer, as you do when you fall for someone. As the July days wore away to August, and those drew to a close, school loomed on the horizon.

I wondered: would this lovely bond stay? Or would it fade, like a summer sunset?

Turns out, I wasn't the only one considering this question.

20

Connor fiddled with his fingers as he looked out at the night sky.

It was his favorite thing to draw because he knew for a fact it was black and white. There was no mounting sense of something missing when he looked at it, no feeling that there was some quality of it that was dulling it for him.

It was what it was.

Connor felt her hand rest on his shoulder.

"Whatcha thinking about so hard?"

Connor smirked and turned to see Iris. She was snuggled on his small twin bed, holding her favorite book. She had come over hours ago, insisting she read him this spectacular novel. He had laughed and relented.

But as she read, Connor found himself becoming.... not jealous, not upset.

Just.... conflicted.

Yes, that was the right word.

Conflicted because he had never known color and would never know it. It wasn't like you could mourn something you've never had.

But Iris deserved someone who would share her love of color with her. Someone who wasn't constantly worried about people finding out.

He had been made fun of at his last school after someone figured out his secret. It was one of the reasons why they had moved. So Connor wouldn't come home, smeared with paint and markers, all colors he couldn't see. So he wouldn't cry and wonder why he had this thrust upon him.

Iris moved closer, wrapping her arms around him.

He smiled and held her arms, tangling his fingers with hers.

"Listen to me: tomorrow is going to be scary. But all awesome things are. We are going to enter school, hand in hand, happy and unwilling to take anyone's ridiculousness. If someone bothers you, I'll sock them in the jaw."

Connor laughed a little. Iris couldn't throw a punch to save her life, but he appreciated the sentiment.

He turned in her arms and looked into her eyes. "I'd do the same for you."

She lifted a brow. "You'd better."

The two laughed. He leaned his forehead against hers.

She sighed, content. "One day I want to tell you something important. Until then, just know that I'm not going anywhere."

Connor smiled, kissed her forehead, and nodded.

He loved her, too.

21

The halls bustled around us as we entered, hand in hand, our colors joining the anxious chorus of high schoolers whose colors danced in nervous waves across the halls. Smiling at each other like dorks, our colors bright in our joy.

That year was going to be one of the best. It was only the beginning.

I don't know where we go from here, after this summer of color.

But I know now my world is brighter with him in it.

Color, like all the best things in life, is best shared.

I can't wait to share more with him.

(But that, that will come much later. For now, like a rainbow, we fade away toward a new day.)

X

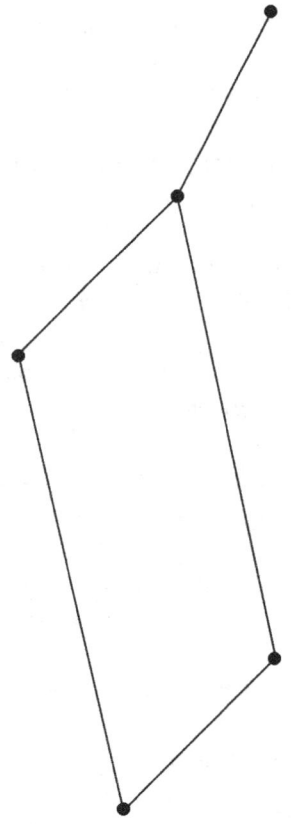

Love seems to be something that comes easily to me.

For some odd reason, whenever I'm stuck on writing something, love or otherwise, my mind wanders to a specific scene:

A couple inside a New York apartment.

The couple themselves have faces I don't recognize. They change almost every time.

Some things stay consistent. The woman is always blonde, the man brunet. She always wears something pink, he's always in a soft blue.

Their apartment has a wall of glass, and the Sun is always shining into their living room.

I'm not sure where they came from, their small sun-lit world coming to me in between thoughts and breaths, growing from a source I never found.

But I'm grateful for them. They have become an endless wheel for stories, their small moments the perfect pictures to transcribe onto the page.

I'm not sure where they came from, or what they mean.

But I'm happy for them, nonetheless.

Not as happy as they are for each other though. That much I'm certain of.

Snapshots

He flips through the album, a grin as bright as the Sun streaming into their apartment.

She has a good eye, always has.

The pictures dance off the page. The two of them on the rapids that one summer.

He stood in one, dressed in a dark blue tux for that charity banquet he made her go to for work, New York moving on behind him.

She smiled in another on Halloween, grinning like a madwoman, holding the axe for her Jason costume.

The two of them, lying in bed, him asleep as her face peaks toward the edges of the frame, the stars winking conspiratorially outside.

She smirked over her shoulder in another as she makes them breakfast, her pink sleep top slipping off her shoulder.

The two of them on the couch, watching the news, hands intertwined as the world bustles on.

She's gaping happily in another, holding up her new typewriter, her knack for pictures working hand in hand with her love of words.

This is their life. It's a few big moments, but mostly its these small moments, these snapshots, that they save.

True, big moments are important to keep track of.

But in the end, when you look back at it all at the snapshots of life, it's the small moments that you remember best.

Of course, those small moments can lead to all that you know about someone, especially a loved one.

This next story is a personal favorite.

The old saying goes "write what you know." I always thought that was lazy or cheating somehow. I also thought it didn't apply to me in some way.

After all, what did I know? Suburbia, normalcy, monotony. No great tragedies or dramatic worlds came to me from the soil of what I knew.

But life is funny like that. You think you know the world around you, know every bone in the skeletons housed in your closets, but then something completely new arrives in a place you thought you knew better than anything.

In this case, it came from my father, who over a candlelit dinner at our favorite Italian place, told me stories of his life I had never heard.

A new skeleton formed, whose bones and shapes I didn't know.

Now I do, and it took me traveling back 50 years and 9,100km, to a place only known through second hand tales and lullabies.

A place people see on TV screens, and like me that night, don't know the bones.

Allow me to assemble them for you.

9,100km

1

Exactly 9,100 km away and many years ago, in a city named Damascus, is the starting point of where two families became one.

Their story is not a tragedy, nor is it simply happy. There are no household grudges or forbidden love. There is war, there is strife, and there is happiness. There are new countries and new lives. There is death and life.

This is a story about two families who became one.

And it starts 9,100 km away.

2

It starts with one man. A man born in a land 9,100 km from the place he now resides. A man who was born when his father went up to his mother, a charming smile on his face and offered her a piece of chocolate. She accepted, they talked, and soon love bloomed.

From that love, their children were born: Four sons and one daughter. They grew up happy, playing soccer and building scooters from wood, a small trick their father taught them. He grew into a man of simple tastes and simple desires. An outrageous thing to be in a world so complicated.

3

And it was getting complicated. War seemed a constant there. Foreigners, men with accents speaking languages he did not understand seemed to flutter around his city. His father knew that language, but never bothered to teach him.

Later, he would learn it anyway.

As time went by, he watched his brother move to a strange land, to study engineering when he really wanted to be a playwright. He came back to visit, but he still seemed a million miles away. Eventually, he stopped coming. The boy who was not quite a man was told his brother is in America.

Soon, he would be on a ship, bound for a land even stranger than the one he thought he knew.

4

Little did he know, years ago, she was on a similar ship, heading to that same land.

She was much too young to realize how big this was. That her parents, her mother, an orphan who fell in love with a dentist (her father), was moving them across the sea. To a new life away from the brewing troubles in a city 9,100 km away. As each one dropped behind, her excitement had grown.

No one ever does know what a new tide will bring.

5

He comes to America, to New York City, finding a rush of lights, people, comeongetamoveonoverhere! Everything whips past him, chaos the normal order of the day.

It reminds him vaguely of home.

He gets work at a jewelry company named Cartier. It's simple work, fixing rings and tuning watches. Giving customers a nice smile as he shows them the new design of the season. He makes friends easily, has an apartment, grabs lunch at a local falafel cart and watches the madness go by.

He makes friends, one in particular with a bright smile and a big heart named Mike. Mike accompanies him around New York, smiling as he, wild and excited, works through the corners of the city, drawing out a map for himself in the madness. Mike stays by him on late nights while he downs coffee in a dingy diner after proclaiming that he has to drive Mike's car. They laugh together when Mike accidentally throws his shoes at a police car than subsequently forgets the next day. They remain together when Mike shows up, humble and contrite, after mistakes that were made in dark moments. They stay friends for many years, "Big" Mike another little constant in his shifted world.

He settles himself, carving out a small chunk of an American life.

6

She grows up in a small apartment in Brooklyn, siblings always on top of each other. Her three brothers and sister always quarreling, always laughing, and always being. She goes to school, learns many things and blushes whenever the boys in the hall spare her more than a fleeting glance. She has many friends, but always goes home after school, the sidewalk well acquainted with her footsteps. She helps her mother cook and clean, smiles when her father comes home from work, a simple world of normal monotony than she is perfectly happy in.

A regular American family. Or as close as they can get.

7

His boss, Mr. Henry, was a kind, eccentric man. Smiling as he sat at the head of the table, the soft music and chatter of the French restaurant spilling around him, he seemed almost an eye in the storm for all the hustle and bustle. It seemed to revolve around him while he himself was a point of calm. He smiled widely as the waiters brought their appetizers. As everyone chatting about their Christmas plans, he saw that each plate seemed to only contain a thumbnail amount of food. He asked, as a joke but also seriously "Could I have the entrée as an appetizer?" Mr. Henry laughed loudly, a bell-like sound that seemed to let the chaos around him rise with jubilation and merriment. He said "Sure, why not?"

He would remember his good humor with a smile and remember how his large appetite and sarcasm always seemed to lead him to good people.

8

His father comes to visit him.

He looks around his apartment, his eyes sharp and critical.

"You can't live like this," he says to his son, eyes distressed. "You need to come home."

He's a dutiful son and does not argue.

He buys a ticket to go back across 9,100 km.

A few days before he goes, his father calls.

"Stay in America a while. Things here are not very good. They've got the draft going."

He understands. He doesn't want a life of war and bullets. His brother tried it for a while but ended up not liking it much.

They were a family of artisans, not warriors.

He thinks he'll stay another year or so.

He ends up staying much longer.

9

He goes to pick up another friend of his one morning for work, by a little house in Brooklyn. It's quieter here, a strange mix of suburbia and city, the two clashing yet mixing well together.

He knocks on the door, and his friend is not the one to open it.

It is her.

She smiles at him, her raven hair seeming to glow in the light. Her smile is soft but has strong edges to it. Her eyes, a warm brown, look at him curiously before she shouts for his friend to come out.

In that moment, he knows that he has met his wife.

10

She isn't too impressed by him.

Sure, he is handsome, and when he begins to show up more, she realizes he is also kind.

He is humble in some ways. Not like the other men she's met, who boast and swagger and preen like peacocks.

He is confident in himself, but also willing to be wrong. A quality that she's rarely seen.

His smile is bright, his hands work worn. He dresses nicely, has a pleasant voice.

She still isn't impressed, though.

(Even though all the little details stick in the back of her mind.)

11

Time passed. A dance with two partners, one taking a step forward, the other a step back. It seemed never-ending, and a few times it ceased all together.

Until finally, both parties took a step forward. And the dance truly began.

...

Her father calls her down one day. He is there, smiling nervously but brightly as always. Her stomach flutters at seeing him.

That was a recent occurrence, but not an unwelcome one.

Her father, a blunt but kind man, gets straight to the point.

"He is asking you to marry him. Will you?"

The question hangs in the air as she looks at him. She sees a good life, not a perfect one, but a good one. One of pitfalls and mountains, good times and bad. But ultimately, a happy life that was worth living, with someone worth living with.

"Yes."

12

The wedding was a day of joy.

She glided down the aisle, her white gown glowing in the multicolored light of the church. He smiled widely, looking at her stride to him on her father's arm, their families and friends smiling happily as she passed. When she got there, the veil revealed her small, secretive smile to him. He gave her one in return as the priest began the ceremony.

When they finally kissed, their secret was open to all: they both somehow knew that this was where they would end up.

13

They got a little apartment in Brooklyn. He worked each day, she did too, jumping from job to job.

Time slipped by, until one day she smiled and told him the news that most hear at this point of marriage.

She was pregnant.

9 months and 18 hours later, a bouncing baby boy named Christopher entered the world with much fanfare and jubilation. His cries would later become a voice of reason and distinction. His eyes filled with ambition and focus. He would soon step before judges and professors and friends and allow his silver tongue to dazzle them.

But that would not be for many years.

14

They moved to another apartment in Brooklyn, this one bigger and better for a growing family.

2 years later, she was pregnant again.

Those two years were tainted, though.

Perhaps it was the universe balancing their otherwise idyllic lives. Perhaps it was the apartment, its wall containing a sinister force that seeped into their days. Or perhaps it was just a bad time, with no true explanation.

Nonetheless, fights broke out between the couple, ugly screaming matches that rattled the floors. Business dropped to a snail's pace, the sparkling diamonds and jewels in his display case (his, he was his own boss now) winking dully at the apathetic eyes that passed them a glance. He didn't think it could get any worse.

He was wrong.

...

She sat, unmoving, unblinking, only registering the traffic down below her.

She sat as a still as a column in that hospital bed, her hands folded before her.

Only hours ago, a baby resided within her, a baby girl she wanted so badly to meet.

Now, nothing.

The technician's furrowed brow at her sonogram should have told her something. The worried look in her doctor's eye when she came to the office with her husband. It all slipped by her until she heard the words.

"Your child's heart has not developed correctly. It only has three chambers rather than four."

The doctor told them of the surgeries, the risk, the poor quality of life the child would have. She had shaken her head, said how she could handle it. She so badly wanted a baby girl, a playmate for her son, another lovely smile, another mouth that called her mommy. Someone she could take about clothes and boys and growing up as a woman with. She wanted it with a fervor that scared her.

But then the baby came. When her screams had subsided, when the doctors waited for that telltale cry, all they received was silence.

They raced, and shouted and tried, but it was too late.

All the while she had screamed in her mind my baby my baby please cry for mama.

In the end, it was inevitable, her doctor said in that sad tone that made her want to howl.

But as she looked down below at the traffic, tracing her now empty belly, visions of big eyes and happy smiles filling her mind, she longed for the opportunity to prove the universe wrong.

15

They left that haunting apartment behind, its dark walls and forbidding air now locked in their rearview.

They move into a brick palace, a split house that shines brightly in spring, a ruby among the stones.

Business picks back up, the lost allure of gems restored to the eyes of his customers.

The unknown tension between him and her ease, bringing them back to familiar serenity.

And finally, on an unremarkable night in July (or day, since it is moments before midnight when this occurs), a baby girl is born.

Their baby girl.

She has shining brown eyes that will forever be lost out windows and in books. A smile that will stretch at the sight of new stories, whether they are bound in hardcover or before her on the technicolor screen of a movie theater.

This little girl adores them. And she will one day, to show that adoration, write a story about them.

16

My family has seen many things.

Things that broke their hearts.

Things that lifted their spirits.

Things that brought tears.

Things that have brought joy.

Things others experience each day, in small doses.

My family is anything but small.

We are loud and proud and sometimes quite crazy.

We have stories to tell in candlelight restaurants and family gatherings that not many have.

We are a family of immigrants who survived the tests of the universe and man, to make it here.

Here, where he, my father, gets to smile at his full-grown son, now a man who is pushing himself to become the best he can be. That ambition became a powerful compass, leading him to the greatness he longs for.

He gets to kiss her, my mother, each morning as he goes off to work, the diamonds dull compared to her smile. She keeps the house they worked so hard to gain, filling it with laughter and food and love.

He gets to hug me, his wide-eyed creation of imagination and hope. And he gets to tell me he loves me.

We are a family.

And I wouldn't have us any other way.

X

Family has always been something that has been around me and with me in everything I do.

Even the family I never got to meet.

The sister I never got to know creeps into my head now and again, a perfect ghost.

Never overly disruptive, never all that solid, yet there just the same.

She makes me remember the beautiful things in life many take for granted, like stars and words and numbers of crows.

Like the little patterns we see each day. Never disruptive, never solid, but there.

This is for the little things that invade my life so wonderfully and for the person who makes me remember them.

And for the little nursery rhyme all writers have heard before.

Too Many Murders (of Crows)

1 for sorrow

More often than
not I try things
at least once.

Because some
never get
even that.

The sorrow
that can come
from every what-if

is more cutting
than any failure.

2 for mirth

I always end
up saying my jokes

twice

because laughter
is free and
everything is funny
the second time around.

(And to see if the invisible
enjoy a good joke)

3 for a wedding

White pages
become placeholders
for dresses and hands
and I *do's*.
I've been to
more than three weddings
but those three things
still end up being
"laters"
for me.

4 for a birth

A little girl
finally in
the world.

Born to loving parents.
and a missing fourth of
a heart.

Maybe that's why
I always try
to organize things
in even sets.

5 for silver

A treasure chest sits
in my drawers at home.

Enough silver
for a ship, a plane, a land
far away.

But if you were here
I'd share every piece
with you.

6 for gold

My father says I have a
heart of gold

I think its
because I have
too much love
stuffed inside.

7 for a secret never to be told

My brother, for all his faults, is a role model
of mine.

His drive always
makes me think
of underdogs and
silver tongues.

Victory you can
taste and grab
with practiced hands.

He does it
effortlessly.

I love him
very much.
But *shhhhhhh........*

8 for a kiss

I will always
remember best
the kisses,
hands,
bee-stung lips,
sweet words,
that
never
really
happened.

9 for a wish

I wish you were more
than a shadow.

More than a what-if.
More than a ghost.

Maybe then I'd know
what only living for one
was like.

10 for a bird you must not miss

I have ten fingers and toes.

They guide me through
grass and cement.

They reach for
love and stars.

They stand me higher
to kiss my father good morning.

They let me write
to you.

(And I hope it doesn't take
more than 10 anything
for you to find this.)

Inspiration for me has come from many different sources.

But each one was preserved against one thing: death.

Death sometimes swallows the best stories, grabbing them from ink stained hands or hushing moving lips, leaving silence in its wake.

Many artists have tried to capture Death in their work, invert the silence by setting it on a stage.

Making afterlives and sprawling kingdoms for after we leave the mortal coil, giving thousands something besides the yawning blackness of oblivion.

But perhaps Death isn't as cruel as we think him.

Maybe like the rest of us, he just likes a good story.

Skeletal Storyteller

In a sitting room
of red and black, white and gold
Death sits and waits
for stories yet untold.

He grins as new people
stop by, spreads his hands
in kind greeting.
Then he gestures for
a beginning, for time
is quiet fleeting.

He hears the
stories each soul
has to tell.
From war to love,
from birth to
funeral bell.

Each one has him entrapped
amazed as each word
hits the air.
He is always stunned
by the richness of life
up there.

The skeletal smiles of the crowd
warm his old bones
as the stories come to an end
the room now silent as stones.

He lets them leave,
off to paradise or hell
as he sits and waits
for the next person

with a story to tell.

Through the stories
Death learns again and again
the beauties of life
and the complexity of men.

So, when you go,
as you grow cold
remember: Death, like us, is happy
to get a good story told.

•

Death hears and takes many stories, but I doubt he always hears the full version of each one right away.

After all, when we go, we leave those we love behind, bits of our stories still clinging to them.

This story talks about those bits, those pieces left behind.

And how many times, many broken hearts collect them, covet them as the days tick on. Hold them tightly so as not to lose them.

(And how sometimes, it is best to let them go. That way all can have rest.)

H.D.D.

1

It's amazing what you remember about people after they are gone.

The little ticks and traits that escaped you until they became all you had left.

Like those little nursery rhymes you used to recite as a kid.

Hickory Dickory Dock.......

Those little things become so important, so vital you weep at the slightest mention of them.

Those little things are what I clung to after my father passed away.

That, and an old antique clock.

2

My father loved little things and old things.

He loved the little nursery rhymes and tongue twisters he kept like bits of paper in his pocket, like a tune you couldn't get out of your head.

He loved running his hands over old clocks, following the paths of its former owners, wondering about their stories.

I wonder if he ever stopped to consider the hands that would come after him.

"Mara."

I look up at my mother, her weary eyes poking from the attic door.

I hold up the clock to her.

She smiles a pained smile.

"He never finished that one. Maybe you can get it working."

I just nod, rise, and wait.
She steps down from the ladder, disappears back into her own grief.

Doesn't bother trying to find the bits of paper, or strain to hear the song.

I hold the clock in my hands and exit the attic.

The clock is silent.

3

The guts of the clock sit before me, brass shimmering in the light of the window and the noon-day sun.

Three days.

Three days and……nothing.

Grumbling, I walk past the kitchen, past the living room where my mother sits listlessly, to the garage.

I search high and low for another screwdriver, maybe a maintenance book, something to help me fix this damn clock.

What I find is my father's log journal. He logged each clock he fixed, who he fixed it for, and a little comment on each one.

Potential portal to an alternate dimension.

Odd croaking noise with no origin.

Beautiful woodwork

I slam the book shut. I leave the garage.

Seeing how he saw each clock, each little detail where others couldn't........I couldn't be reminded of that right now.

I return to the clock.

It remained silent.

4

Judy watches me from across the room, tapping her pen against her notepad.

She's nice, and definitely a good therapist. But I doubt I'm her favorite patient.

For one thing, she has to pull teeth with me.

"How are you, Mara?"

Thumbs up

"How has your week been?"

Shrug

Like I said, pulling teeth.

I'm just not good at, well......talking.

Just like my dad.

"Tell me about this clock your mother mentioned, Mara."

I don't want to say anything, because I can't stand the ideas she'll spout. About how this is a coping mechanism, how this is something I'm doing to feel close to my father.

It hurts to hear, hurts to narrow the yawning chasm in my chest as something to simply be dealt with.

The reprieve (and dare I say magic) the clock brings with it, with each wire I fix and every inch I clean, revealing the designs beneath, chopped down into just a coping mechanism, something unhealthy and dramatic that needs to end at some point.

Time, like grief, is infinite to me. It doesn't go away so easily. You can't pause time, and you can't make pain smaller.

So, I stay quiet.

Silent as the clock.

5

The fairy's painted smile at the top of the clock is mocking me.

Her lips create that same little pout my mom used to have on when I said something ridiculous as a child.

Before the accident, before her lips stayed frozen in an ever-present thin line.

I want to talk to her, want her lips to unfreeze and smile at me again.

But we don't always get what we want. We make compromises.

So, for another day, I stay silent.

Silent as the clock.

6

My father was always so composed when he was working on a clock.

No matter how frustrating the problem appeared, he kept his cool.

At times outside of the clock, the same could not be said.

It's hard to reconcile the angry giant with my loving father at times.

But I'd take his anger over the silence in my house right now.

The source of it seems to be the clock.

Cold, silent, and dead.

Just like my dad.

7

My mother is humming.

Not anything specific, just snatches of notes that she weaves together with air and sorrow as she cooks dinner.

But she's still humming.

It's something.

It fills the silence the clock seems in no hurry to shatter.

8

That stupid rhyme.

It keeps sticking into my mind, winding and slipping between my ears like a fly.

My dad would mutter it playfully as his hands flew around his table. The clock ticking right as he finished the last dock.

I try muttering it like a wizard summoning some power. Maybe for a minute, just one minute please, he can come back to me and tell me how this damn clock is supposed to work.

Hickory Dickory Dock

The mouse ran up the clock

The clock struck one, the mouse was done.

Hickory Dickory Dock.

Nothing.

Nothing.

More blasted, stupid nothing!

With all the strength I have, I heave the block of wood down on the table. It stays fine, stubbornly held together as I weep.

Daddy, please. Please don't be done. I miss you.

9

"Mara!"

"Mara, sweetie, don't cry!"

"Please talk to me, love, shhhh, don't cry."

"Mama's here, please talk to me, baby."

"I want Dad!"

"Oh sweetie. I know you do. I miss him every day. I miss the way he'd make the house smell like clock oil and sawdust. How he'd say those silly rhymes to you whenever you helped him with his clocks. How he would tell you stories about each one. How he'd only eat potatoes if they were boiled. How he hated pop music. Honey, I miss him every day. I know you do too. I'm sorry I haven't said anything until now."

"It hurts!"

"I know, sweetie. It's going to for a while. You have to remember to let it out. You can't just keep bottling it up. You have to let these things out. They're like the gears of a clock. They need to come out in order for the clock to be fixed.

"I love you, sweetie. I'm so sorry I wasn't there to help you. I've got you now, sweetie. I love you."

"I love you too."

10

Judy was smiling sadly at me as I finished recounting my break with my mother.

"Mara, I'm so sorry you've been hurting like this. But, I'm glad you're ready to move forward. The process may seem long, but it will be worth it."

I nodded, considered, then said "Thank you, Judy. For actually giving a shit."

Judy laughed. "Well, I wouldn't be any good at my job if I wasn't. Now, how's the rest of your week been?"

I take a breath, the first one that hasn't felt like something was out a place in a long time.

I was finally ticking. And tocking. And moving forward.

11

As it turns out, the problem was right there. I just wasn't able to see it, focused and blinded as I was.

The clock was just jammed. Nothing that couldn't be fixed.

I closed the latch on the back, wound it up, and off it went.

Mom smiled as she placed it on the mantle. Hugging me, we both watched as the clock ticked on between the tinsel and fairy lights,

the Santa statue and the angel
Dad loved to place at the very end.

Tick.

Tock.

Tick.

Tock.

Tick.

Tock.

On you go, hickory.

Dickory.

Dock.

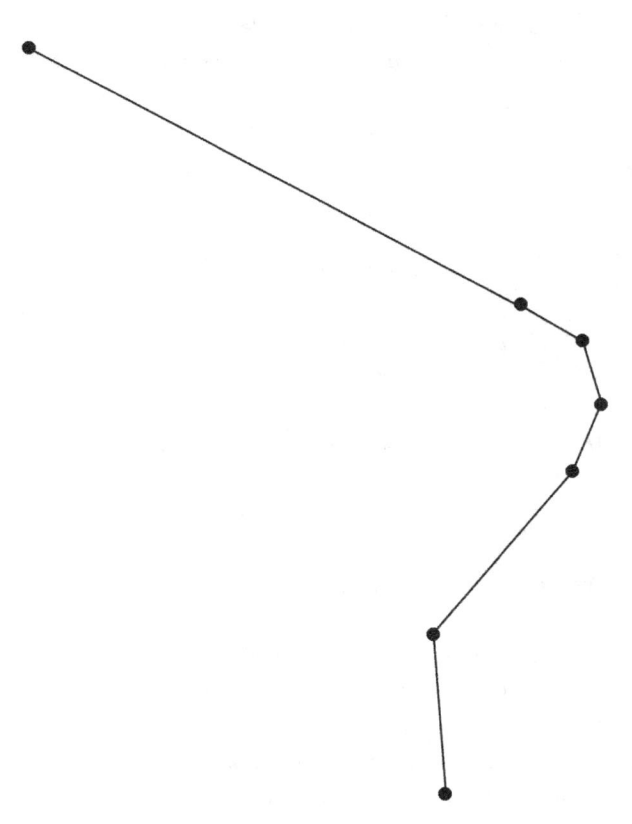

I think the reason why Death seems so fascinating to me, and the rest of humanity, is what goes on in the realms of Death.

Religions of every kind have paved with golden words the ancient battle for as long as humanity has existed.

Good and Evil.

Right and wrong.

Salvation and Punishment.

Such concepts have haunted, inspired and downright reformed our minds and the way we look at stories.

There is always some great battle, some horrible enemy to slay.

But what if there wasn't?

What if it was less a battle and more of a misunderstanding?

And what if the supposed good guys actually realized they had messed up? Acted too rashly, rendered judgment too quickly?

Those ideas gave birth to this piece. A what—if many don't seem to consider, and a task even the most divine struggle with:

Saying you are sorry.

Swallow

Down I went
down
                        the
                                                winding
            tunnels
   that
                        had
no
end.

I arrive to find him.
Clad in red
lounging lazily
on his alabaster throne.
I wince as I spot
the crown of thorns
and the crimson blood
that drips
drips
drips
down his angular face.
The screams of the damn sound
louder than Heaven's choirs
The Devil stands.
His orbs stay lifeless, cold.
Those pools that once lit
the skies
now hold nothing.
Those eyes stay boring into me
as his voice scratches over my ears:
"Why are you here?"
The walls seem to close around me
waiting for an answer.
I try to summon the words
words I held within on the way down

words that say what has been
grossly overdue.
But they stick
in my throat
held by the toxic honey
of too much power
and pride.
Like father, like son.
I turn to go, defeated by my own damned righteousness.
But as I do, the honey slips away
and the words held
come out a whisper.
"I am sorry."
He does not hear,
back already turned from me.
Some things are just too little
too late
But that does not make
it any easier
to swallow.

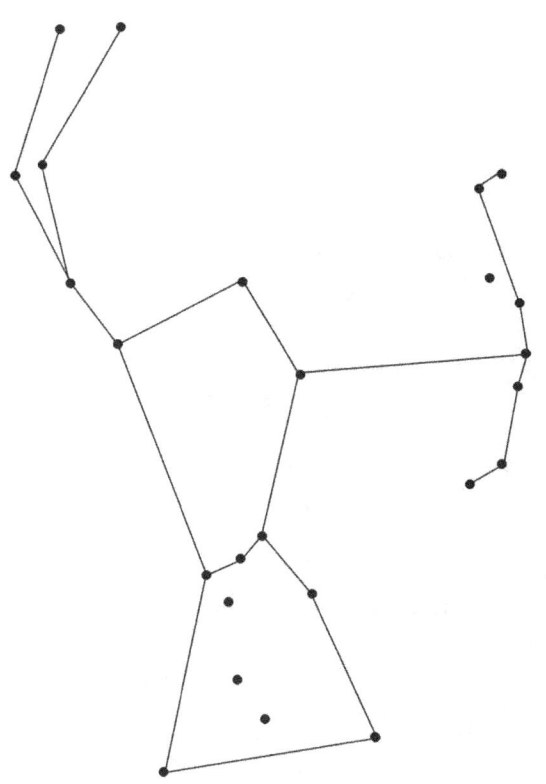

Something like that must haunt an immortal mind, I think.

That regret, that want to fix and redo is so human, but imagining it on the divine is somehow a blasphemy.

Aren't we made in the image of the divine? So, aren't they allowed to be as flawed as we are?

Aren't they able to appear in places and in ways conventional minds would find ill fitting?

For me, divinity, good, evil, and mortality are all nebulous concepts, as plentiful as fruit in the fridge or grass on my lawn.

So, this was born, popping up among the masses.

Dancing with Devils and Other Such Nonsense

She grew up with verses and holy oil, old books proclaiming the world to be as black and white as her favorite bakery treat.

She grew up thinking that you don't dance with the Devil unless you're heading to Hell anyway, which she was not, no sir.

Until she got out of the chapel one day and saw him.

Leather and shocking blonde hair, piercing eyes and a bad attitude. That's all she was able to glean that first time.

The second time, she was close enough to see his broken halo, shattered but gold is gold. It still glitters no matter the state of it.

He was a terrific dancer, that much she was certain of.

Her feet never burned past the lovely ache of long hours pounding the floor, her eyes never filled with any hellfire.

Because she always scoffed at old sayings anyway, because the world she was shown by him is fuller of color than any book could capture.

Despite what the demons in cardigans said as they clutched their books and turned their backs, she was not going to Hell, no sir.

She looked into his eyes and found out that devils make good dance partners of every kind.

While some say she sinned, she will always swear up and down she figured out Heaven that night like it was a math problem.

It took some time and a bit of effort, but like all good things it was worth it.

She got better dance moves, but never forgot the rhythm and rhyme of the book she grew up with, going each week and holding her head high.

He still remained a Devil to the core, but like all people he mellowed as the years ticked on, his steps still lively but his eyes warmer, kinder from both life and love.

He was, and always would be, a devil of a dancer though.

Decently good husband too, though such nonsense was never said.

(But it was still seen, and no angel in Heaven could deny there was a kind of backwards holiness to the whole damn thing.)

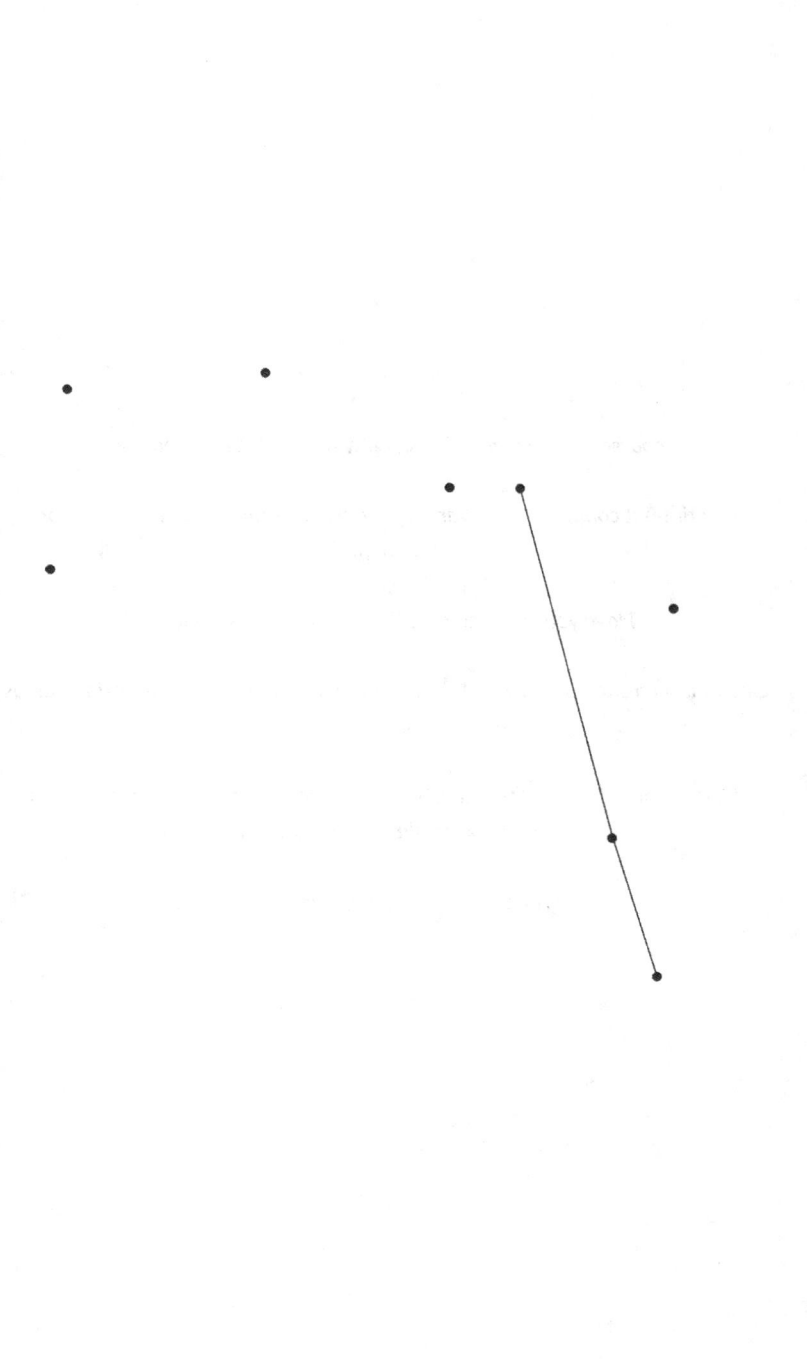

Of course, godly inspiration isn't always needed for good poetry.

Sometimes it comes with no warning and from a source so small many don't bother to find it.

Have you ever had a really good idea in the shower?

One that seems to babble out of the running water and hit your ears and hair as you shampoo?

That happens to me quite often, but sometimes I'm too slow to catch them before they slip down the drain.

This is one of the few drops I was able to save.

Shower Thoughts

I'm not sure how it
happened but you
seemed to have wormed

your way into my head.
Eyes as sunken as the ships
at the bottom of the sea

limbs akimbo, rigor mortis gripping tight
already, Death never one to
procrastinate.

I wonder when the staccato
BANG BANG BANG
will come, grim faced

police arriving, voices cutting
into my mind, waiting for
it to unravel in tears
and madness, Poe rolling

over in his grave
as I show them
the ink covered
carcass on my desk.

Writers can be cruel
gods some days
and no amount of

holy water or showers
can cleanse them of
their need for a

pound of inky flesh.

My family paved the way to find what I loved. But those weren't the only stories and moments I looked to for inspiration as the years went on.

As I said, inspiration comes from the oddest places. For me, another plentiful source grabbed me from the shelves of the mythology section of my library in middle school.

I've loved mythology ever since, the ancient stories that chronicle the creation of the world, its many heroes and deities with noble hearts or wandering eyes.

Their stories and songs always carried a magic within them, their might having survived the test of time, as polished and beautiful as they were in the days of old.

The fact that that shine continues today, easily remolded and refitted for new ideas and versions, is amazing to me.

It proves some things truly are immortal.

And some stories are too good to die.

So, here is my tip of the hat to those above and below who run the cosmos we all know and love.

And what better way to tip the hat than a poem, a luxury of the days of old that has also withstood time's challenge?

Pocket-Sized Gods

1.
The great ruler of Olympus
who never seems to keep it
in his toga.

Thunder cracks
and I wonder

who pissed you off
this time.
 It seems your lightning

has worked its way
to my fingertips.
They sting

with the need to touch
someone, anyone
but unlike you

I have no one
to caress.

2.
The patron of artists,
the man who makes
that glowing circle

keep on going.
I'm sorry I
yell at you

when I can't think
of any new stories.

But you're an artist,
I figured you
would be somewhat
sympathetic.

3.
God of the underworld
Lord of the dark.
I wonder if you like

the hundreds of stories
we've written about you
and your wife.

I'm as guilty as the rest
but understand we lonely souls
see your love

and see possibility.

The sweet whispers of
the dark will always
be better than
sitting in the Sun

choking on prayers.

4.
The octopus creation
of a man fearful of everything.
Your existence makes me shutter

not because of your face
(I love calamari)
but because you

are a giant opposition
to my optimistic view
of our universe.

Jagged stars striking
out of a blackened sea
where you reside.
Now I stay up at night

wondering if it holds
compassion or apathy.

And that is scarier than any
monster I've ever known.

5.
You need no introduction.
Our society has worshipped you
long enough it doesn't matter

that we can't pick you
out of a crowd.
I remember my mother

dragging me to
your house every Sunday.
But I didn't find you

with the saints, but
the sinners, rocking

out to Joan Jett
and singing showtunes.

And as a member of
your flock, who
am I to not
sing along?

6.
Goddess of war
your name is
pounded into your
footsteps upon the dead.

Your dance is deadly
in ways not allowed by
the world across the sea.

You remind me
that I can be
powerful beyond the
swing in my hips
and what's between
 my thighs.

and that war is never
just a man's game.

7.
Skin of amber.
Eyes of emerald.
Hair aflame.

A goddess from a
forgotten age
grown from in-between

my thoughts. You are
the person I aspire to be.
Fearless, strong, passionate

kind and wise. You
are the best parts
of me

in a form
that isn't afraid
to show them.

Cheers to these pocket-sized gods
that I carry with me.
Who give me their thoughts
and stories.

Without them,
I would have never
made my own.

It makes sense that my thoughts of good, evil, divinity, love, and destiny would stem from such a simple love of the few dots I can see from my driveway on any clear night.

Like the stars, my stories and thoughts are vast and go on even when the eye can no longer make anything out in the dormant sky.

Some of those stories have fallen into these pages like comets.

Others still hang above, waiting for their chance to be seen.

For now, here is one last bit of light that decided to forgo the spots above my driveway and make their way to you.

All These Little Stars

Every night that I can, I stand outside in my driveway and count.

One,

        Two,

                Three,

Four,

        Five,

                      Six,

            Seven,

    Eight.

Eight little stars.

Now, eight stars is not impressive to look at.

It's not like in the movies where the stars fill the sky.

Twisting and touching each other like lovers as the night slips by.

It's mostly a few dots filling a vast, empty space.

A space not many people give much thought of outside of prose and romance.

But I love those eight little stars.

I crane my neck each night to see them when the clouds decide to rest from their hovering.

Why?

Because those little stars remind me of the little things I love in my life.

They stand as the music I love to listen to.

The beats pumping through my veins like blood, like magic.

They are my family, ever present and bright as I go through my life.

They stand as the love I hope to one day give.

It goes on the page rather than pouring into another heart

(for now, and I wish on those stars each night for the day to come sooner.)

They are the faith I hold in the universe.

A beautiful mosaic made by god(s) whose artistic eye I will always tip my hat to.

They stand as the words of poets and writers I've loved.

Whose words helped me begin to build my own works from the ground up.

Giving me foundation to build my own temples to the written word.

They are all that I have experienced and seen in my short life.

Memory that not even Death can silence.

Only watch as the stories tell and retell themselves over and over again.

They are the stories I've told to you today, here in this book.

Their words hopefully giving you what you hoped they would.

And they are a reminder that though you only see these now, there is a galaxy of stories out there.

And I intend to explore them.

I love all these little stars I have been given and give to the universe.

So, here's to those stars.

To what I will give and be given in the future.

Hopefully, those little stars will soon connect into a vast, glowing sky,

bright,

wonderful,

and ever shifting.

Fin

I suppose I should wrap this up.

Much as I'd like to continue, the rest of the stars have faded, and morning is on its way.

I suppose you'd expect me to close on some fantastic note that wraps up everything nicely.

A thought you keep in mind at the end of the book to take with you after you closed it and move on with the morning.

But again, I never really was much for standards and how things are done.

So, for now, I'll just end on a good old fashion goodbye.

Make of that, like the stars and the universe, what you will.

About the Author

Nicole Zamlout is a young author who is currently studying at The College of New Jersey for English. She has had fascinations with storytelling and poetry her whole life, and hopes by the end you find some fascination with it as well.

A List of Constellations

Ara
Lyra
The North Star
Horologium
Orion
Pyxis
Ara

A Note To Our Furious Readers

From all of us at Read Furiously, we hope you enjoyed our newest title, *All These Little Stars*.

There are countless narratives in this world and we would like to share as many of them as possible with our Furious Readers.

It is with this in mind that Read Furiously pledges to donate a portion of our book sales to causes that are special to the publisher. These causes are chosen with the intent to better the lives of others who are struggling to tell their own stories.

Reading is more than a passive activity – it is the opportunity to play an active role within our world. At Read Furiously, we wish to add an active voice to the world because we believe any growth within the company is aimless if we can't also nurture positive change in our local and global communities. The causes we support encourage a sense of civic responsibility associated with the act of reading. Each cause has been researched thoroughly, discussed openly, and voted upon carefully by Read Furiously.

To find out more about who, what, why, and where Read Furiously lends its support, please visit our website at
readfuriously.com/charity

Happy reading and giving, Furious Readers!

Read Often, Read Well, Read Furiously!

Look for these other great titles from

Poetry
Silk City Sparrow
Dear Terror
Whatever you Thought, Think Again
Until the Roof Lifted Off
Chocolate Brown Satin Hot Pants and Other Artifacts
Heirlooming
And She Does Shine

Essays and Anthologies
Furious Lit vol 1: Tell Me A Story
The World Takes: Life in the Garden State
Putting Out: Essays on Otherness
Working Through This

The One 'n Done Series
Helium
Brethren Hollow
Girls, They'll Never Take Us Alive
What About Tuesday

Graphic Novels
Pursuit: A Collection of Artwork
In the Fallout
Brian & Bobbi
The MOTHER Principle